My Cup
of
Tea

My Cup of Tea

of

Tea

Sam Twining

JAMES X JAMES

Contents

1 Legends and Some Basic Facts

Boiling tea, 1617.

Scholars taking tea in a bamboo garden in 15th-century China.

Tea stretches back into the mists of time and the Chinese and Japanese have some wonderful legends about its origin. One such legend says that Emperor Shen Nung, the son of a princess and a heavenly dragon, was one day downwind of a burning camellia bush, and much liked the delicious aroma it gave off. Tracing the source it was he who discovered tea, cultivated it and introduced it to his people. Another legend says that in 2737 BC Emperor Shen Nung (who must have been a model ruler) found it was only safe to drink boiled water. Out for a picnic one day, whilst boiling his water – very conveniently for him and for us – the leaves of a nearby tree fell into the boiling water and so he discovered tea. A third legend surrounding Buddhists claims that Bodhi Dharma or Bodhidharma, a saintly man, had taken on the task of devoting seven years of contemplation of Buddha in 500 AD somewhere in India. Becoming sleepy he tore out his eyelids and where they touched the ground two tea bushes appeared; quickly revived by the tea he completed his task!

Some early legends tell of monkeys being used to collect tea leaves from inaccessible trees; others tell of an Emperor's annual

Monkeys plucking tea in China.

tribute being picked by monkeys. There are even people around today who will tell you monkeys pick the best tea!

Whatever you may believe, there is no doubt that tea was first found growing wild in what is today the western province of China, Yunnan; but the first recorded cultivated tea bushes – bushes pruned by man rather than wild tea trees – were recorded in 350 AD in the hilly district of Szechwan. Tea drinking became so popular that cultivation spread down the Yangtze valley and then along the coast. By 900 AD it had reached the Singlo hill district in Anhui province and the Bohea hills between Fukien and Kiangsi provinces.

The Chinese accepted the medicinal values of tea as early as the 4th century AD. Tea was consumed throughout Chinese society by

Lidded porcelain tea mug,
Chinese, 1979.

Facing page: a Geisha in traditional dress performs the Japanese tea ceremony.

the time Lu Yü wrote *The Classic of Tea* in the 8th century AD. In 593 AD Buddhist monks took their knowledge of tea growing and the Chinese tea ceremony, which involved 24 articles of tea equipage, to Japan which remained cut off from the rest of the world until fairly recent times. One could say that today, when we see the Japanese tea ceremony, we are looking at a virtual re-creation of how the Chinese prepared and drank their tea all those years ago; but the Chinese on the mainland moved on and today drink their tea either from a bowl poured from a teapot or a delightful lidded mug or from a guywan (a Chinese covered bowl with saucer).

The first Chinese tea leaves were brewed in open pans, but during the Ming dynasty (1368–1644 AD), it was found that steeping the processed leaves in hot water produced the most flavourful results. This meant the tea needed to be kept hot during steeping, so a lidded vessel was created to retain the heat. A type of ewer normally used for wine was adapted for brewing tea, and from this evolved the teapot, fashioned from the white translucent porcelain made by the Chinese as early as the Tang dynasty (618–906 AD).

The Chinese are great horticulturists who discovered that tea is like wine: not in any alcoholic sense, but in obtaining its character and flavour from the soil in which it grows and being affected by the height at which it is grown and, of course, the weather in which it is grown.

Over a period of time the Chinese developed green tea, which is picked from the same bush as other teas but is not oxidised, making it light and very thirst-quenching. They developed red tea (called Oolong) which is partly oxidised, and black tea which is fully oxidised and therefore has much more colour and pungency. There is also white tea, made from very small buds and leaves plucked in early spring; little is made and even less sold outside China. Using the

Some examples of the tokens used by London coffee houses because of the shortage of small change, a large number of which were issued in the 17th century.

Facing page: a Mughal painting of a European man with his servants, early 17th century.

Customers in the coffee house in Salisbury market place, 1782. Cartoon by Rowlandson.

wine simile, we may think of green tea as white wine, Oolong as rosé and black tea as red wine. All tea in China originally came from Camellia Sinenis, a cousin of the camellia plant. Indian tea comes much later in this story (see Chapter 3).

The earliest reference to tea by an Englishman is in 1615 in a letter between two agents of the East India Company. The first recorded advertisement for tea in Britain was

Left: 19th-century tea trade in China.

Above: left to right, coffee from Arabia, tea from China and chocolate from the Americas, 1688.

in *The Gazette*, no. 432, from Thursday, September 2nd to Thursday, September 9, 1658: 'That Excellent, and by all Physitians approved, China Drink, called by the Chineans, Tcha, by other Nations Tay, alias Tee, is sold at the Sultaness-head, a Cophee-house, in Sweetings Rents by the Royal Exchange, London.' Tea has to thank the London coffee houses for its introduction, in competition with coffee, chocolate and alcohol. Garraway's Coffee House, in Exchange Alley, London, founded in 1657 by Thomas Garway, sold tea in leaf form in 1660

from 15s. per pound. An Act of Parliament that year levied a duty of 8 pence per gallon of liquid tea sold, raised in 1670 to 2s. per gallon.

In 1662, the drinking of tea gained royal approval. The Portuguese, the great navigators, were the first Europeans to reach China and it was they who brought tea back to Portugal. It was not well received, but, luckily for us in Britain, the Portuguese princess, Catherine of Braganza, liked it. She is believed to have brought tea in her dowry when she arrived at Portsmouth in 1662 to marry Charles II. As Queen, she made tea fashionable in the London Court.

It was not until 1669 that the East India Company imported tea for the first time – 143½ pounds! By 1678 it had risen to 4,713 pounds. The next part of the story is hard to believe. Tea had many enemies, in the form of the clergy, doctors and brewers. The clergy said that, as tea came from a heathen country, it was a sinful drink. Doctors said it was bad for you. And far, far worse, brewers lobbied the government and claimed that tea would replace ale at breakfast!

This was a wonderful excuse for the government to gain extra revenue, and so in 1698 a duty of 5s. per pound was imposed. The earlier tax on the coffee houses of 8d. per gallon, later 2s. per gallon, for liquid tea was dropped, being too expensive to collect because by this time there were over 2000 coffee houses in London alone.

Thomas Garway's teas (see Chapter 1) were selling at between 16 and 50s. a pound, but when Thomas Twining (1675–1741) bought Tom's Coffee House and specialised in tea in 1706, prices were generally a little less: Bohea 16s. to 24s., Pekoe 24s. to 30s., green tea (Hyson) 14s. to 20s. per pound. There is some evidence to show that black teas like Bohea came from China first and that green teas such as Hyson a little later. Amongst the black teas were Flowery Pekoe, Orange Pekoe, Pekoe Souchong, Souchong, Congou and Bohea. Green teas included Gunpowder (so called because British merchantmen thought this tea looked like lead shot, and so the name has stuck all these years), Imperial Hyson, Singlo, Bing and Caper.

It is interesting to note how some of these teas obtained their modern names, especially when the British are notoriously bad at languages. Char, tschai, tscha, tay but we call it tea!

Pekoe: 'pak-ho', two Chinese words meaning literally 'white hairs' around the edge of the young buds of tea.

Souchong: 'siau-chung', means little plant.

Congou: 'kong-fu', meaning labour in preparation of the hand rolled leaves.

Bohea: 'wu-i' from the mountains of Fukien.

Hyson: 'yu-tsien', before the rains.

Singlo or Twankay: the Hyson shrub improved by cultivation on the Singlo mountain.

Tea was of course grown in many parts of China but it was the south east provinces that exported tea.

Thomas Twining was very aware that no lady would be seen dead in a coffee house! The ladies who were his customers had to wait outside in their sedan chairs or carriages, sending in their footmen to buy the tea. When Thomas could afford it during the first ten years of trading, he would acquire a small house next door. By 1717 he

Facing page: 'Mr and Mrs Hill', painting by Arthur Devis, c. 1750. The possession of tea and its equipages was a status symbol

Above: a Tea Garden, engraving published 1790.

Facing page: a full set of 18th-century tea drinking equipment.

had three such houses which he then converted into a dry tea and coffee shop, which he called the Golden Lyon, selling a wide range of best-quality teas and coffees. This was the first such shop in the western world where ladies could enter without any impropriety. He also wholesaled tea to coffee houses, apothecaries, inns, milliners and one grocer! Thomas Twining's shrewd move from coffee house to retail shop was in line with the times for ladies were trying to suppress coffee houses in favour of tea gardens which were much more civilised. So coffee houses disappeared or changed themselves into men's clubs, some of which remain today in Pall Mall or the vicinity of St. James's. Tea gardens varied from small places of tranquillity to famous venues such as Vauxhall and Ranelagh. Tea and other refreshments were enjoyed, but it was expensive. Ranelagh charged two shillings and sixpence per person. Though tea gardens continued into the first half of the 19th

century, they gradually lost their original lustre and became no place for society. The tea gardens were in turn replaced by something else but that comes later in this story.

Now we must go back to how our tea ceremony started. We know that all the original tea bowls and teapots were Chinese. The ladies fell in love with this translucent material, even being painted with a tea bowl in the hand, held by the thumb underneath and two fingers on the rim, leaving the little finger, the pinky, at an affected angle. Ladies of the time were anxious to show off their own delicate bone structure and whiteness of skin compared with the Chinese porcelain. There is nothing like a little vanity. They would also like to show off that they could afford to have tea and all its equipages.

Potters in Britain were keen to enter the tea-ware market and at first made use of traditional earthenwares and stonewares. The earliest British teapots are of reddish-brown stoneware and date to the last few

Left to right: agateware
teapot, 1745–50; salt-glazed
stoneware tea jar, 1750s;
creamware teapot, c. 1770.

years of the 17th century. A pair
of Dutch brothers, John and
David Elers, settled in north Staffordshire
and began producing such wares, decorated
with applied sprigged motifs in the Chinese
style. By c. 1720 white salt-glazed stoneware
was being used for teapots and, to compete
with imported Chinese porcelain, British
potters developed a range of novelty glaze
effects. These mimicked the qualities of
precious stones and were given such names
as 'agateware' or 'tortoiseshell ware'. Later
earthenware was shaped into brightly
coloured pineapples, melons and even
cauliflowers. In the 1760s Josiah Wedgwood
perfected a cream-coloured glaze for earthenware and his 'Queen's ware' (named in
honour of Queen Charlotte) was sold in
large quantities at home and abroad.

And yet all the time British potters were
striving to perfect a porcelain body to rival
the Chinese imports. There was great exper-
imentation and recipes were closely guarded

secrets. By the 1750s they had
successfully created a type of 'soft
paste' porcelain which was white and
could be decorated in the Chinese manner.
But there was a problem. This 'soft paste'
porcelain was fired at a relatively low temperature and was not always heat resistant. If hot
water was poured there was always the
danger of the teapot shattering. At the time
these were called 'flying teapots' and few
survived. Customers were advised to warm
their teapots gradually before pouring in
quantities of hot water. It is thought that tea
drinkers would also put a little milk into
their tea bowls to avoid them shattering: the
legendary origin of 'MIF' – milk in first! In
fact there are records of milk in tea much
earlier.

The problem was resolved when Plymouth
chemist William Cookworthy registered the
use of 'china clay' and 'china stone' in 1768.
These were the vital ingredients for
successful 'hard-paste' porcelain which,

Top: porcelain 'soft paste' teapot, 1790. Above: pearlware teapot, c. 1800–5.

Left: the Countess of Boufflers taking tea in her boudoir, 1760.

Below: a George III caddy in the shape of an apple, c. 1800.

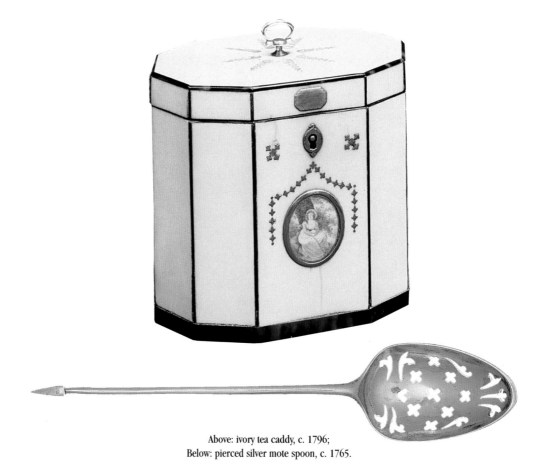

Above: ivory tea caddy, c. 1796;
Below: pierced silver mote spoon, c. 1765.

26

when fired at a higher temperature than 'soft paste', would withstand hot liquids. The expiry of Cookworthy's patent in 1796 meant that anyone was free to make porcelain, leading to a boom in production. In the early years of the 19th century a fine 'bone china' (using ground animal bone) was developed and crafted into elaborate tea services. The basic recipe is still used today by manufacturers of elegant tableware.

Not only did one require considerable funds to purchase tea, a pound being equivalent to a skilled craftsman's weekly wage, but besides the teapot, bowls and their saucers, there were other necessities. Mote spoons date from as early as 1697. Made of silver, having small holes in the ladle and with a long thin shaft and a point at the other end, these were issued to each guest, so as to genteelly remove the floaters. The point or spike was for the use of the hostess, literally inverting the spoon handle down the spout to unclog the leaves, rather like a ramrod.

(There is some evidence that early shipments of Chinese teas arrived unsorted so that a mixture of large and small leaves would clog the spout and create floaters.) Teaspoons eventually replaced mote spoons when tea strainers came into use between 1790 and 1805 and teapots started to have integral strainers inside at the base of the spout. If you had a tea caddy you would also have had a caddy spoon made of silver, although some were made of a variety of materials such as treen, gold, tortoiseshell, fruitwood, hardwood, glass, brass, silver plate, shell, mother of pearl, ivory, bone, horn, coconut, pewter, jade or Blue John. Caddy spoons evolved from the fact that the Chinese put a real scallop shell as a scoop at the top of every chest, box, tub or pot of tea they exported. The silversmiths could not resist this idea which is why the early caddy spoons were shaped like a shell. Long-handled caddy spoons date from c. 1745, short more popular ones date from c. 1770.

Above: the dangers of not knowing the etiquette of the teaspoon, 1825. Cartoon entitled 'A Tea Party or English Manners and French Politeness'.

'A Frenchman not aware of the custom constantly returned his cup without the spoon in it, which being immediately replenished by the lady of the house, he thought it a point of politeness to drink the contents which he continued to do, to the great surprise of the company until he perceived the lady pouring the 14th cup, when he rose in great agony and cried Ah! Madame, excuse me I can take no more.'

'Le Thé à l'Anglaise' by Olivier. A society concert at the house of the Princesse de Conti, mid 18th century .

And so it came about that the lady of the house would take the key from the chatelaine and unlock her tea caddy. It always had two containers, later canisters, one for black tea (usually Bohea) and the other for green tea (usually Hyson or Gunpowder Green). She would do this only once or twice a week to show off to her neighbours, friends and relations that she had tea in her home!

Between the tea containers, if the caddy was handsome enough, would be a glass mixing bowl to blend the two teas, if that was required. Otherwise the teas would have been taken on their own. The caddy spoon would have been used to weigh out what was equivalent to gold dust, to mix it if required in the mixing bowl, and then to measure the tea into the teapot. The caddy spoon was normally kept in the locked caddy. Either a silver tea kettle with spirit burner would provide the hot water or a Sheffield-plate hot water urn would be used, a servant bringing a red-hot iron from the kitchen fire to be

lowered into the urn to boil the water. The lady of the house, having made the tea, poured it into bowls standing on saucers, each with a silver mote spoon, and passed each serving out to her guests. White sugar would have been offered; it was expensive too, and in some households it was kept in the tea-caddy mixing bowl, to keep it away from the servants. Although there is a record of sugar tongs made to look like fire irons as early as c. 1720, they changed to be sugar nippers, and by c. 1770 became elegant sugar tongs. Milk seems to have been offered from the early 1700s. In some households there was even a special jug for it. It comes up again in the history of tea during the 'flying teapot' period (see page 24), but milk was not taken seriously until the pungent, malty teas of Assam, India started entering Britain in 1839.

Above left: porcelain teapot, Thomas Rose, Coleport, Shropshire, c. 1805; right: silver sugar tongs, 1794.

Facing page: Chamberlain's Worcester tea service, c. 1795–1800.

3 Tax and Less Tax

Richard Twining I, grandson of Thomas Twining, recommended the abolition of duty on tea.

Facing page: 'The Cultivation of Tea in Assam' from *The Graphic*, 1875.

The tax on tea rose to 119 per cent and lasted until 1784. It was so high that many people bought tea from smugglers. Holland was now supplying half the tea sold in Britain. Many tea merchants went out of business, refusing to sink into illicit practices. Others adulterated tea with leaves of ash (called smouch), liquorice or sloes, even sheep dung was used on occasions. Because green tea was easier to adulterate, black tea gained in popularity. By 1725 convicted smugglers were fined £100, and in 1766 imprisonment was introduced.

The Boston Tea Party of 16th December 1773, which this book must exclude, set minds thinking. Between 1768 and 1783 imports averaged 5.8 million pounds with 50 per cent *ad valoreum* duty plus 1*s*. 1*d*. per pound. Tea sold at auction at the average price of about 4*s*. 6*d*. per pound became over 7*s*. 6*d*. per pound with duties added. William Pitt the Younger, on forming his first Government in 1783, was determined to investigate taxation. Mr Pitt honoured Richard Twining, grandson of Thomas Twining (see chapter 2) and the elected Chairman of the London tea dealers, with several meetings. Richard Twining recommended the abolition of duty on tea, with tea merchants paying a lump sum to make up the lost revenue for four years. However, the Commutation Act of 1784 reduced the tax to 6½*d*. per pound. A window tax was introduced to protect the revenue, which did not suffer, but increased so much that the window tax came off again.

So 1784 is really the year we in Britain became the tea-drinking nation we are today, but all done on China tea – there was no other. And humans being humans, having mostly been denied tea, badly wanted to have it, and they did – fulfilling the prophecy of those brewers a century earlier, because tea did replace ale at breakfast! The price of tea fell. Tea merchants were happy, smugglers ceased to trade tea and teapots got larger. The consumption of tea rose from £5.8 million in 1768 to £10.8 million in 1785.

TEA GARDENS, CHERIDEO

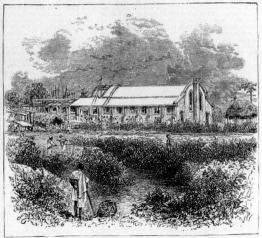

TEA HOUSE, MAZINGAH

A BRIDGE—VASSANGOR DISTRICT

WOMEN PLUCKING TEA, MAKEEPORE

TEA GARDENS, GALAKEE

INTERIOR OF A TEA HOUSE

Above: Anna Maria Stanhope (1783–1857) as a child, and right, as the lady-in-waiting who probably introduced afternoon tea to the young Queen Victoria.

Facing page: afternoon tea.

Below: Queen Victoria at tea with her family in the garden at Osborne, Isle of Wight, 1887.

There is some evidence that tea was taken in the afternoon by a few people prior to the Victorian age, as tea bowls gave way to cups around 1810. There is a splendid legend concerning Anna Maria Stanhope (1783–1857) which is well worth recounting. Anna married the 7th Duke of Bedford. She was unusual in that she designed her own jewellery and clothes. She became a little peckish between the much earlier lunches of those days and the much later evening meals. She is credited with having the idea of taking tea to drink and a few nice delicate things to eat in her drawing room and so invented afternoon tea. She became the Lady of the Bedchamber to the young Queen Victoria in 1837, and doubtless suggested this novel idea of afternoon tea to the Queen, who set the fashion.

Charles, 2nd Earl Grey (1764–1845), became Prime Minister in 1832. He gave his name to what is today the most popular of all speciality teas.

Above: Earl Grey, 1824, who gave his name to the most popular of all speciality teas.

Above top: a grand porcelain teapot, 1835.

Facing page: high tea, quite different to afternoon tea.

Previous page: Victorian idyll – a cliff-top picnic.

This is the age of full tea services with the teapot as the centrepiece. Some teapots in the full Romantic style became so grand, one imagines they could strut across the elegant tea table. 'Afternoon tea' became a sophisticated meal, and the tea service manufacturers and silversmiths enjoyed extra business. We must not confuse 'high tea' with 'afternoon tea'. Factory workers and others returning home sat at a high table to have their most important meal of the day – tea to drink, a meat dish, bread and butter and jam – and much later supper, consisting of biscuits and cake and tea to drink. Many homes still serve high tea and many midland and northern bed and breakfasts do the same today.

In 1826 John Horniman invented the first packet tea which he test-marketed in the Isle of Wight. Grocers would not handle it but chemists and confectioners would. Later,

when other 19th-century tea blenders started up, the packets had a health message on them for this reason.

In the early 19th century wild tea was identified growing in Assam in north-east India. Chinese seed was brought in and failed in Assam, but was to do much better later on in Darjeeling, in the foothills of the Himalayas and in southern India. The local plant was tried and the first of this new tea, Assam, was auctioned in London in 1839. Because it was from a British colony no duty was imposed. This tea was stronger, more pungent and maltier than any previous tea from China. Anyone who did not take milk already would have done so now.

Chinese tea had been manufactured by hand but Indian tea was caught up in the Industrial Revolution and machine-made. Just two leaves and a bud are plucked, then withered all night to remove excessive moisture. It is then rolled, to twist and release the enzymes – the more rolling, the smaller the leaves become when oxidisation commences which will later give the tea its flavour. Oxidisation continues in a carefully controlled room where the enzymes literally brew up; it is critical that this process be stopped at just the right time. The leaves are then put into a rotating oven where all organic reaction ceases and where the heat deactivates the enzymes, thus stopping the oxidisation. The enzymes and juices are dried onto the surface of the leaves and the carbohydrates (sugars) in the leaf are partially caramelised. The tea is then sorted into leaf grades, and when sufficient weight of a type is collected, it is sent to auction. Production of tea has altered little since those days, with the exception of a change in the Second World War, which we will come to shortly.

In the northern hemisphere tea is grown from March to November or early December. When the tea bush has been dormant or in periods of restricted growth, fine flavour and quality is often the result. Conversely when the weather is warm and wet, higher production and plainer quality is

Above. left to right: fish teapot, c. 1880; Royle's patent self-pouring teapot, c. 1890; Oriental dwarf holding a mask, c. 1876. All made in England.

Facing page: Sri Lankan tea pickers.

Below: Horniman's tea advertisement. In 1826 John Horniman invented the first packet tea.

Lyons Corner House 'nippy' preparing tea, 1930s.

Lyons lorry in India.

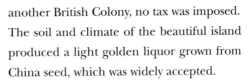

another British Colony, no tax was imposed. The soil and climate of the beautiful island produced a light golden liquor grown from China seed, which was widely accepted.

Tommy Lipton, who started a grocer's shop in Glasgow, bought land in Ceylon in 1890 to produce his own tea, bypassing the London auctions in Mincing Lane. The co-operative movement pre-dates Lipton, first importing tea in 1883. Brooke Bond dates from 1892, as does Mazawattee, a name that has now disappeared. Typhoo dates from 1905. The tea trade was going through growing pains,

Tea advertisements. Clockwise from top left: Brooke Bond, Mazawattee, Ty-phoo, Co-operative Wholesale Society and Lipton's teas.

Above: Ceylon tea
packet, 1884.

Below: the 'simple yet
perfect' teapot
invented by Lord
Dundonald, c.1905.

Facing page: a tea
table as illustrated in
Mrs Beeton's cookery
book (1907 edition).

as the older tea companies still sold loose tea. The new ones sold packet tea, which grocers generally distrusted, hence many packets carried health messages. Advertising and promotion was being used more and more and consumption in Britain was to reach 258 million pounds in 1901, a huge increase from 53 million pounds fifty years earlier.

Tea packing was done by hand. Packets, made up from a sheet of lead foil, were placed in a 'block', a hollow wooden brick, with one end open. The empty packet was inserted and filled with tea using a funnel. Once filled, the open end was folded down and a three-piece label stuck over both ends and one side. The price and weight were normally printed on the ends. Another method was using pre-made paper bags, sealed with a small glued paper square, and printed with weight and contents.

Later the 'Rose' machine was invented. This was loaded with two reels of paper, one being an inner liner, while the other (often coloured) formed the outer wrap. The machine cut the paper into rectangles, and folded and shaped it so the tea could automatically be filled, and the open end folded over. The machine then stuck a three-panel label on, ensuring both ends were sealed, and the main face would be decorated with the packer's name and details of the blend it contained.

At about the time that packet tea was becoming better established, the 'simple yet perfect' teapot was invented by Lord Dundonald. Whilst it never caught on, the idea of infusers did. Today there are many types: some fit as an integral part of the teapot, others are accessories to be hung inside the teapot. As long as they are not made of aluminium, and are large enough to allow the loose tea to swell and infuse properly, they are quite acceptable.

From an advertisement introducing the tea bag.

There are two stories about the origin of tea bags. The Americans like to claim that in 1908 a New York tea broker sent his samples out in little silk bags which inadvertently ended up in someone's teapot or cup without opening, and so the tea bag was invented. However, the French have a counter-claim that they were sewing tea in little muslin bags at the turn of the century and so invented the tea bag! Tetleys tried them in the USA as early as 1935. The war years made materials difficult to obtain and so they re-started after the Second World War. Other companies followed suit and today tea bags are with us in many shapes and sizes. But remember – from a home economics point of view, if you have the time, loose tea is still the best buy. Many British homes have both, using tea bags when in a hurry, or only one person is having tea, but when you have time and company it is always best to use loose tea.

From top: earthenware teapot, c. 1931; earthenware moulded as a racing car, c. 1938; 'Cosy' teapot with aluminium cover, 1940s; 'Fine Way' teapot, 1994.

Tea in the 20th Century and Today

The Edwardians enjoyed huge breakfasts, breakfast teas and later tea dances. London's Waldorf Hotel introduced the tango in 1913; tango teas followed and tea dances only stopped in 1939 because of the War.

In the USA iced tea is claimed to have been invented in 1904, at the St. Louis World Trade Fair, but the Chinese may well have invented it years before. To make good iced tea, use a high grown Ceylon tea or tea bag. Make one teaspoon or bag stronger than usual. Fill a pitcher with ice, having put a little sugar in first. Pour the hot tea over the ice, top it with cold water, put it in the fridge, and only garnish it before you serve it with a bruised mint leaf, slice of lemon or cucumber or a bruised borage leaf. Today iced tea accounts for the major part of US consumption. Ready-to-drink teas started in 1992 in the USA and have come to Britain.

By 1961 British consumption reached 9.9 pounds per head per year, the highest ever, but in the Second World War strict rationing allowed only 2 ounces per week!

Tea dance, Brighton, 1930s.

The Second World War. Tea fuelled every aspect of the war effort. Right: a mobile canteen serves tea to workers and survivors on a bombsite. Below: an RAF planning meeting.

Facing page:
'Conversation piece at the
Royal Lodge, Windsor,
1940' by Sir James Gunn.

Above from the left, tea at: the Four
Seasons, London; the Prince of Wales,
Niagara on the Lake, Canada; Browns, and
tea dancing at the Waldorf, both of London.

Trying to save shipping space, the British Government encouraged tea planters in India and Ceylon to convert to lower-density tea. This was achieved by producing 'CTC' (cut, tear and curl, an invention of the 1930s) which smashed the leaves, forming a granular appearance and producing quick colour tea. Being a nation of habit, we have it today, but less is consumed thanks to tea bags (see Chapter 4). After the Second World War tea growing spread to east Africa and later to South Africa and South America, and today is found in many more countries.

Many third world countries have started to drink tea. Using boiling water can even improve general health. Western-style countries tend to drink less tea, but of better

Left from the top, tea at: George V, Paris; Pierre, New York. Below: Hilary Clinton battling for health care reform, 1993.

Facing page: tea at the Ritz, London.

quality and greater variety. Green tea has had a revival, but has yet to reach the popularity it enjoyed years ago.

A tea man is neither a medicine man nor a scientist but it is safe to say that tea is good for you. Research increasingly suggests that both green and black teas might play a role in the prevention of a number of cancers and heart diseases. As evidence continues to build, the precise benefits will be more iden-tifiable. Organic tea is in demand, and whilst naturally more expensive, will continue to grow in popularity. To keep tea or tea bags fresh, store them in a screw-top jar or tea tin. Tea, like blotting paper, draws up kitchen smells and moisture. Black tea has a longer life than green tea, so buy the latter more frequently.

Looking at . . . Iguanodon
A Dinosaur from the CRETACEOUS Period

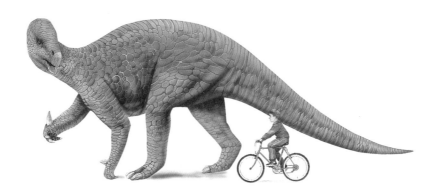

THE NEW
DINOSAUR
COLLECTION

For a free color catalog describing Gareth Stevens' list of high-quality books, call 1-800-542-2595 (USA) or 1-800-461-9120 (Canada). Gareth Stevens' Fax: (414) 225-0377.

Library of Congress Cataloging-in-Publication Data

Amery, Heather.
    Looking at-- Brachiosaurus/written by Heather Amery; illustrated by Tony Gibbons.
        p. cm. -- (The New dinosaur collection)
    Includes index.
    Summary: Describes the physical characteristics and probable behavior of this long-necked dinosaur.
    ISBN 0-8368-1044-9
    1. Brachiosaurus--Juvenile literature. [1. Brachiosaurus. 2. Dinosaurs.] I. Gibbons, Tony, ill. II. Title. III. Series.
QE862.S3A437 1993
567.9'7--dc20   93-25687

This North American edition first published in 1993 by
Gareth Stevens Publishing
1555 North RiverCenter Drive, Suite 201
Milwaukee, Wisconsin 53212 USA

This U.S. edition © 1993 by Gareth Stevens, Inc. Created with original © 1993 by Quartz Editorial Services, Premier House, 112 Station Road, Edgware HA8 7AQ U.K.

Consultant: Dr. David Norman, Director of the Sedgwick Museum of Geology, University of Cambridge, England.

Printed in the United States of America

3 4 5 6 7 8 9 99 98 97 96 95

Looking at . . . Iguanodon

A Dinosaur from the CRETACEOUS Period

by Jenny Vaughan

Illustrated by Tony Gibbons

THE NEW
DINOSAUR
COLLECTION

Gareth Stevens Publishing
MILWAUKEE

Contents

Introducing
Iguanodon

Imagine you could travel back in time to 120 million years ago. What creatures would you see? What did planet Earth look like then?

It was the age of the dinosaurs. Among the many different kinds that roamed the world then was **Iguanodon** (IG-<u>WA</u>-NO-DON). It lived in a part of the globe that is now known as Europe at a time scientists call the Cretaceous Period.

The world then was much warmer than today, even at the North and South poles.

Iguanodon was a very large animal with a long, strong neck. It was about four times your height and lived in groups or herds. You  could have recognized it by its beaked face and spiked thumb. You probably would have found it quite frightening.

But was it really dangerous? How much do we know today about this giant prehistoric creature? Turn the following pages to find out.

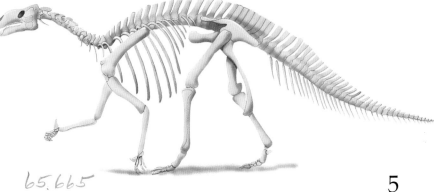

65.665

5

Portrait of Iguanodon

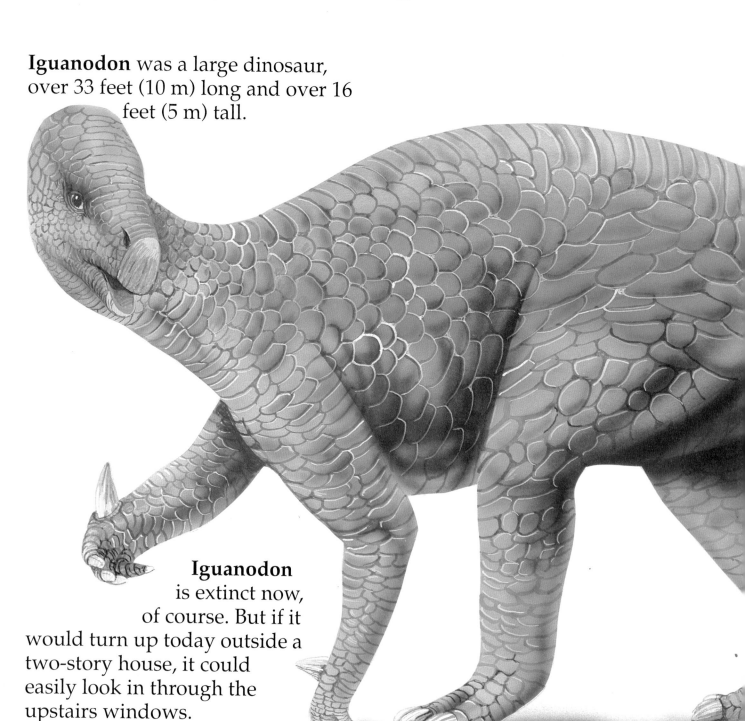

Iguanodon was a large dinosaur, over 33 feet (10 m) long and over 16 feet (5 m) tall.

Iguanodon is extinct now, of course. But if it would turn up today outside a two-story house, it could easily look in through the upstairs windows.

We know that **Iguanodon** ate plants. Scientists can tell this by looking at the shape of the remains of its teeth, which it used to grind food.

Iguanodon's teeth were shaped much like those of a modern reptile, the iguana. But they were a lot bigger. There were 50 or more lining each jaw. **Iguanodon** also had a sharp, hornlike beak, which it used to cut and nibble at leaves. It was a little like the beak of a tortoise.

Iguanodon's front feet worked like hands. Its little finger on each front limb was especially useful. It could use this finger to grab juicy leaves and pull them toward its mouth. Scientists think **Iguanodon** could also use its hands for walking.

Although it was a plant-eater, **Iguanodon** was strong and could fight off enemies. It had a sharp spike on each hand instead of a thumb, which it used to defend itself from predators like the savage, meat-eating **Megalosaurus** (MEG-A-LOW-SAW-RUS).

But **Iguanodon** probably did not fight very often. When danger came, it could run away quickly on its long back legs and find refuge from its enemies.

As it ran, it probably held out its tail, straight and stiff, behind it.

A young **Iguanodon** could run much faster than you can.

Massive skeleton

A large number of **Iguanodon** skeletons have been discovered in Germany, England, and Belgium. Scientists have learned a lot about **Iguanodon** from studying its bones.

Iguanodon's skull was long and thin, giving it an elegant, slim face. **Iguanodon's** massive body left lots of footprints and tracks in mud.

The skeleton shows us, for example, how big and powerful **Iguanodon** must have been. **Iguanodon** had a long, strong backbone with short spines all along it under the skin. Its tail was long and straight. Scientists think that male and female **Iguanodon** probably looked very much alike, but the males may have been larger.

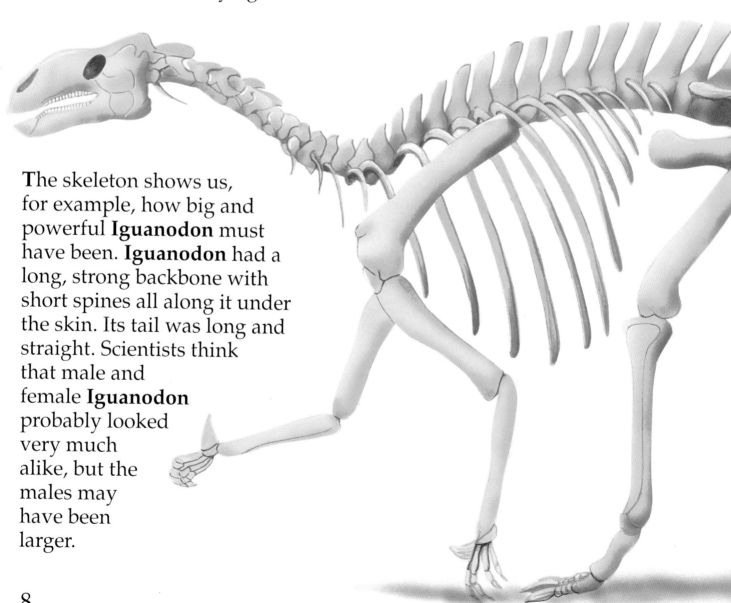

8

From these, we know that **Iguanodon** possibly lived in herds. The young stayed in the center, and the adults patrolled to protect them from predators.

Scientists believe that when **Iguanodon** was young, it walked on its back legs most of the time. But, as it got older, the front legs grew very heavy, and **Iguanodon** found it easier to move around on all fours.

Smaller **Iguanodon**, standing on their back legs, were nimble and had the speed to run away from large predators. But fully grown **Iguanodon**, with their heavy forelimbs, could not have moved quite so fast and would have relied more on their size and strength to fight off vicious meat-eating enemies.

At up to 33 feet (10 m) long, and with a sharp thumb spike for use in close combat, **Iguanodon** would have made other dinosaurs think twice before attacking.

Iguanodon had three toes on each foot. It walked on these in the same way that an emu does today.

Iguanodon belonged to a group of dinosaurs that had hips like those of birds. Other dinosaurs had hips like those of lizards.

Iguanodon's world

The world in Cretaceous times was very different from our planet as it is now. Even the land and seas were in different places.

And many trees and flowers known today did not exist then. On land, there were many kinds of dinosaurs that shared the landscape with **Iguanodon**.

Iguanodon lived in warm, marshy places in swamps and lakes, where there were crocodiles and turtles, too. Large, meat-eating dinosaurs, like **Megalosaurus**, were savage predators and often a threat. But some, such as **Hypsilophodon** (HIP-SEE-<u>LOAF</u>-OH-DON), were small. Others, like **Pelorosaurus** (PEL-<u>OH</u>-ROE-<u>SAW</u>-RUS) in the distance, were big but not dangerous because they were plant-eaters.

11

Iguanodon's day

An **Iguanodon** herd was browsing among the giant ferns and horse-tails. The animals spent most of their time looking for food, like all large plant-eaters, and were busy chopping off leaves with their sharp beaks.

Shrieking with alarm, the herd tried to run away. They could move quite rapidly – up to 22 miles (35 km) per hour. But the **Megalosaurus** was faster and soon caught up with them.

Suddenly, a meat-eating **Megalosaurus** sprang out of the bushes. It wanted a meal.

Megalosaurus's stomach was rumbling with hunger. It grabbed an **Iguanodon** in its mighty claws and prepared to sink its teeth into its throat.

But the **Iguanodon** fought back to protect itself, using its deadliest weapon – the daggerlike spike that it had on each hand. It plunged both spikes into the predator's hide. The meat-eater yelled out in pain.

The **Iguanodon** now returned to the herd and spent the remainder of the day resting and eating with its family. Now and again, the herd moved on – the older **Iguanodon** lumbering on all fours, the younger ones running along on their long back legs. One of their number had been lucky and had a narrow escape from death.

The **Iguanodon** stabbed again and again at the ferocious attacker that, by now, was bleeding furiously. At last, the **Megalosaurus** gave up and limped off. It would have to wait for a meal.

But they all had to remain alert in case of another attack.

13

A great discovery

Mary Ann Mantell was the first person to find **Iguanodon** remains. She lived in Sussex, England. In 1822, she accidentally found a huge, strange tooth among some stones that workmen were using to mend holes in the road.

Mary Ann Mantell's husband, Gideon, was a family doctor but also an expert on fossils. (These are the remains of plants and animals that lived millions of years ago.) He was fascinated by the tooth his wife had found.

Gideon Mantell could not identify the tooth and wondered which creature it belonged to. Soon, he found more strange teeth and some bones in the quarry the stones had come from.

One bone, he noticed, was sharp and very pointed.

He showed the bones to a group of paleontologists (scientists who study fossils). They said they were rhinoceros bones or possibly those of a giant fish. But Gideon Mantell thought they were wrong. He was sure the bones came from an extinct creature of some kind.

The teeth he found seemed to be like an iguana's. This led him to believe they must have belonged to a huge, extinct relative of the iguana. And so he gave **Iguanodon** its name, which means "iguana tooth." In many ways, an iguana does look like some dinosaurs. Its skin has scales, and it also has sharp claws.

Gideon Mantell thought the sharp, pointed bone had originally belonged on **Iguanodon's** nose, like a horn. But, today, we know it was **Iguanodon's** thumb, used as a spike to defend itself against predators.

The Iguanodon dinner

On New Year's Eve, 1853, a dinosaur expert, Sir Richard Owen, gave an unusual dinner party in a park in London, England.

About twenty scientists sat down to enjoy a lavish banquet inside an **Iguanodon**. The meal was delicious. Mock-turtle soup was on the menu, followed by pigeon pie and mutton cutlets.

Never before had any of the scientists been inside an **Iguanodon**! There was not a lot of room, and they were very cramped.

But this was not a real **Iguanodon.** It was a life-sized model, made by a sculptor named Waterhouse Hawkins.

Because the model **Iguanodon** was not quite finished, the guests could sit inside. Together, they all drank a toast to what they thought was an accurate model of **Iguanodon**.

Sir Richard Owen had told Waterhouse Hawkins what he believed **Iguanodon** looked like when it walked the Earth, but he was not quite right. He thought **Iguanodon** must have looked like a giant rhinoceros, with a spike on the end of its nose.

Of course, we now know that the spike was on **Iguanodon's** hand and was used as a weapon.

Many of Owen's models still exist today and are on display in a park in southeastern London. It was Sir Richard Owen who first thought up the word *dinosaur*, meaning "terrible reptile."

OWEN

MANTELL

17

Trapped!

Over 100 years ago, miners in Bernissart, Belgium, found some giant bones while digging for coal. Scientists studied them and soon realized the bones were the remains of a group of adult **Iguanodon.**

The scientists were puzzled, however. There were nearly 30 **Iguanodon** skeletons in all. They thought the dinosaurs must have all died at the same time. So what had happened to cause their deaths?

At first, it seemed that a herd of **Iguanodon** may have been feeding together in a ravine by the side of a river. It might have been raining so hard that a great deal of water poured into the ravine. The herd was busy enjoying a meal, so perhaps the animals did not notice what was happening until it was too late. Scientists thought this was one possibility.

Today, however, some experts think it may not have happened quite like that. There may have been a lake in the area that is now Bernissart in Belgium. From time to time, dead **Iguanodon** may have been washed into it, becoming buried in the mud on the bottom of the lake after a while.

Millions of years then passed. The mud in the dried-up lake slowly turned to rock, and plants became today's coal. Then, by chance, in 1878, the Belgian miners came across what turned out to be **Iguanodon** bones – 985 feet (300 m) below the ground.

19

Iguanodon data

Scientists believe that **Iguanodon** first appeared on Earth about 125 million years ago in the Cretaceous Period. Generations survived for about 20 million years before finally dying out.

Although **Iguanodon** was large, it was not the biggest of the dinosaurs that walked the Earth. For example, the meat-eating **Tyrannosaurus rex** (TIE-<u>RAN</u>-OH-<u>SAW</u>-RUS <u>RECKS</u>) was 6.5 feet (2 m) longer. But they would never have met. **Tyrannosaurus rex** also lived in the Cretaceous Period, but several million years after **Iguanodon** had already died out.

Head and beak

Iguanodon had a long head with a broad beak at the front of its mouth. This was made of bone with a covering of horn. Its edges were sharp and could snap off tough twigs. The beak was self-sharpening.

Mighty tail

When **Iguanodon** walked along, it held its long, stiff tail straight out behind it to provide balance. It had rows of tendons – like strings – along the bones of its back to help with this.

20

Cheek teeth

Iguanodon had a row of teeth on the side of each jaw. As **Iguanodon** moved its jaws, these strong cheek teeth would grind its food.

Scientists believe **Iguanodon** stored its food inside its cheeks until it was ready to enjoy a meal. Then it would swallow and digest its ground-up vegetarian meal.

Thumb spike

Iguanodon's thumb spike was a deadly weapon. **Iguanodon** used it like a dagger to stab through the thick skin of any dinosaur that tried to attack it. The spike was mainly for self-defense.

Finger hooves

Iguanodon's front limbs were very unusual. The little finger could bend easily, and **Iguanodon** could use it to grasp twigs and leaves. In the middle of the hand were three hooved, flat fingers that bent outward, instead of inward as your fingers do. **Iguanodon** may have used them for walking.

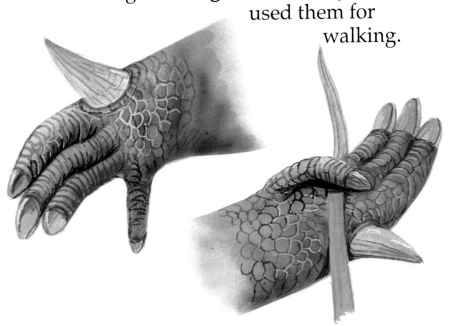

The Iguanodontid family

Iguanodon belonged to a family of dinosaurs called **Iguanodontids.** They all had teeth like **Iguanodon's.**

Iguanodon (1) was the biggest member of the family. It lived almost throughout the northern part of the world. A great many skeletons have been found in England, Germany, and Belgium.

Ouranosaurus (OO-<u>RAN</u>-OH-<u>SAW</u>-RUS) **(2)** was a smaller cousin and lived about 110 million years ago. **Iguanodon** was nearly extinct by then. Bones belonging to **Ouranosaurus** have been found in Niger, in western Africa. It was about 23 feet (7 m) long and looked a lot like **Iguanodon** except that its head was longer and flatter. It had what looked like a sail on its back.

Ouranosaurus lived in the desert. The sail helped it take in heat from the Sun in the morning.

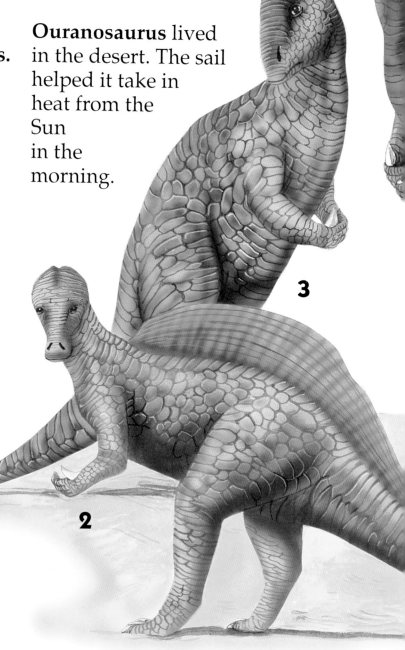

3

2

Later, as the day grew hotter, the sail could give off heat and cool **Ouranosaurus** down.

Probactrosaurus (PRO-<u>BAC</u>-TRO-<u>SAW</u>-RUS) **(3)**, another cousin, lived at about the same time as **Ouranosaurus**.

But it was smaller still – only about 20 feet (6 m) long. It lived in what is now Mongolia, Asia, and looked very much like **Iguanodon**, too.

Muttaburrasaurus (<u>MUT</u>-A-<u>BUR</u>-A-<u>SAW</u>-RUS) **(4)**, another relative, was about the same size as **Ouranosaurus** and was named after Muttaburra, in Australia, where some of its bones were found. It first appeared on Earth about 105 million years ago, when **Iguanodon** was already extinct. So, it was really a descendant rather than a cousin.

Some scientists believe that, unlike any other members of this family, **Muttaburrasaurus** ate meat as well as plants. It may have attacked other dinosaurs for food or perhaps fed on the remains of other dead creatures.

1

4

23

GLOSSARY

emu — a large Australian bird that cannot fly.

extinction — the dying out of all members of a plant or animal species.

herd — a group of animals that travels and lives together.

hide — the skin of an animal.

nimble — able to move quickly and lightly.

predators — animals that kill other animals for food.

refuge — a place of shelter or safety.

remains — a dead body or corpse.

reptiles — cold-blooded animals with hornlike or scaly skin.

skeleton — the bony framework of a body.

INDEX